◨ READERS

Level 2

Dinosaur Dinners
Bugs! Bugs! Bugs!
Slinky, Scaly Snakes!
Animal Hospital
The Little Ballerina
Munching, Crunching, Sniffing, and
  Snooping
The Secret Life of Trees
Winking, Blinking, Wiggling,
  and Waggling
Astronaut: Living in Space
Twisters!
Holiday! Celebration Days around
  the World
The Story of Pocahontas
Horse Show
Survivors: The Night the
  Titanic Sank
Eruption! The Story of Volcanoes
The Story of Columbus
Journey of a Humpback Whale
Amazing Buildings

Feathers, Flippers, and Feet
Outback Adventure: Australian
  Vacation
Sniffles, Sneezes, Hiccups,
  and Coughs
Starry Sky
Earth Smart: How to Take Care
  of the Environment
Ice Skating Stars
Let's Go Riding!
I Want to Be a Gymnast
LEGO: Castle Under Attack
LEGO: Rocket Rescue
Star Wars: Journey Through Space
MLB: A Batboy's Day
MLB: Let's Go to the Ballpark!
¡Insectos! *en español*
¡Bomberos! *en español*
La Historia de Pocahontas
  en español
Meet the X-Men
Spider-Man: Worst Enemies

Level 3

Spacebusters: The Race
  to the Moon
Beastly Tales
Shark Attack!
Titanic
Invaders from Outer Space
Movie Magic
Plants Bite Back!
Time Traveler
Bermuda Triangle
Tiger Tales
Aladdin
Heidi
Zeppelin: The Age of the Airship
Spies
Terror on the Amazon
Disasters at Sea
The Story of Anne Frank
Abraham Lincoln: Lawyer, Leader,
  Legend
George Washington: Soldier, Hero,
  President
Extreme Sports

Spiders' Secrets
The Big Dinosaur Dig
Space Heroes: Amazing Astronauts
The Story of Chocolate
LEGO: Mission to the Arctic
NFL: Super Bowl Heroes
NFL: Peyton Manning
NFL: Whiz Kid Quarterbacks
MLB: Home Run Heroes: Big Mac,
  Sammy, and Junior
MLB: Roberto Clemente
MLB: Roberto Clemente
  en español
MLB: World Series Heroes
MLB: Record Breakers
MLB: Down to the Wire: Baseball's
  Great Pennant Races
Star Wars: Star Pilot
The X-Men School
Abraham Lincoln: Abogado, Líder,
  Leyenda *en español*
Al Espacio: La Carrera a la Luna
  en español

A Note to Parents

DK READERS is a compelling program for beginning readers, designed in conjunction with leading literacy experts, including Dr. Linda Gambrell, Professor of Education at Clemson University. Dr. Gambrell has served as President of the National Reading Conference and the College Reading Association, and has recently been elected to serve as President of the International Reading Association.

Beautiful illustrations and superb full-color photographs combine with engaging, easy-to-read stories to offer a fresh approach to each subject in the series. Each DK READER is guaranteed to capture a child's interest while developing his or her reading skills, general knowledge, and love of reading.

The five levels of DK READERS are aimed at different reading abilities, enabling you to choose the books that are exactly right for your child:

Pre-level 1: Learning to read
Level 1: Beginning to read
Level 2: Beginning to read alone
Level 3: Reading alone
Level 4: Proficient readers

The "normal" age at which a child begins to read can be anywhere from three to eight years old, so these levels are only a general guideline.

No matter which level you select, you can be sure that you are helping your child learn to read, then read to learn!

LONDON, NEW YORK, MUNICH,
MELBOURNE, AND DELHI

Series Editor Deborah Lock
Art Editor Clare Shedden
U.S. Editor John Searcy
Picture Researcher Liz Moore
Jacket Designer Emy Manby
Production Angela Graef
DTP Designer Almudena Díaz
Illustrator Peter Dennis
Subject Consultant Peter Bond

Reading Consultant
Linda Gambrell, Ph.D.

First American Edition, 2006
Published in the United States by DK Publishing, Inc.
375 Hudson Street, New York, New York 10014
06 07 08 09 10 10 9 8 7 6 5 4 3 2 1

Published in Great Britain by Dorling Kindersley Limited

DK books are available at special discounts for bulk purchases for
sale promotions, premiums, fundraising, or educational use.
For details, contact:
DK Publishing Special Markets
375 Hudson Street
New York, New York 10014
SpecialSales@dk.com

Library of Congress Cataloging-in-Publication Data
Hayden, Kate.
Starry sky / written by Kate Hayden.-- 1st American ed.
p. cm. -- (DK readers. Level 2, Beginning to read alone)
Includes index.
ISBN-13: 978-0-7566-1959-6 ISBN-10: 0-7566-1959-9 (pbk)
ISBN-13: 978-0-7566-1960-2 ISBN-10: 0-7566-1960-2 (hc)
1. Stars--Juvenile literature. 2. Astronomy--Juvenile literature. I. Title.
II. Dorling Kindersley readers. 2, Beginning to read alone.
QB801.7.H395 2006
523.8--dc22
                                    2006006441

Color reproduction by Colourscan, Singapore
Printed and bound in China by L. Rex Printing Co., Ltd.

The publisher would like to thank the following for their kind
permission to reproduce their photographs:
Position key: a-above; b-below/bottom; c-center; l-left; r-right; t-top
Alamy Images: Mary Evans Picture Library 24tl, 25tr; Picture Contact
26b; Royal Geographical Society 7; **Norbert Aujoulat / Centre National
de la Recherche Scientifique / CNP-MCC**: 4; www.bridgeman.co.uk:
27t; British Library 17t; **Corbis**: Claudius / Zefa 11b; Stapleton Collection
9; **DK Images**: Anglo Australian Observatory 20; British Museum, London
17b; NASA 1, 30b, 30-31b; NASA / Hubble Heritage Team 21cl; **NASA**:
CXC/SAO 31t; ESA and The Hubble Heritage Team (STScI / AURA)
21cr, 21bl; H. Ford (JHU), G. Ilingworth (UCSC / LO), M. Clampin
(STScI), G. Hartig (STScI), the ACS Science Team, and ESA 21br;
Robert Williams and the Hubble Deep Field Team (STScI) 21t; **Science
Photo Library**: J-C Cuillandre / Canada-France-Hawaii Telescope 3; Dr
Fred Espenak 19b; MPIA-HD, BIRKLE, SLAWIK 12r; NASA 18-19t;
David Nunuk 5b, 32cra; John Sanford 32t; John Sanford & David Parker
11t; Jerry Schad 22b, 24-25b; Dr. Jurgen Scriba 32clb; Eckhard Slawik 5t,
10b, 15, 16, 23, 27b, 29tl, 29tr; Frank Zullo 14br, 28t
All other images © Dorling Kindersley
For more information see: www.dkimages.com

Discover more at
www.dk.com

Contents

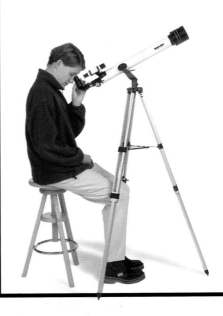

DK READERS

BEGINNING
TO READ ALONE
2

Starry Sky

Written by Kate Hayden

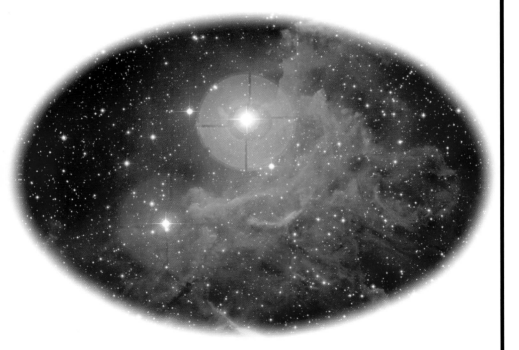

DK Publishing, Inc.

On a clear, dark night, the sky
sparkles with thousands of stars.
These giant balls of gas make
their own heat and light
just like our closest star, the Sun.

Long ago, when people lived
in caves, they noticed patterns
among the brightest stars.
They made them into pictures.
If you look up into the sky,
you can see star patterns, too.

*Stars drawn
onto the wall
of a rock shelter
in France
16,500 years ago*

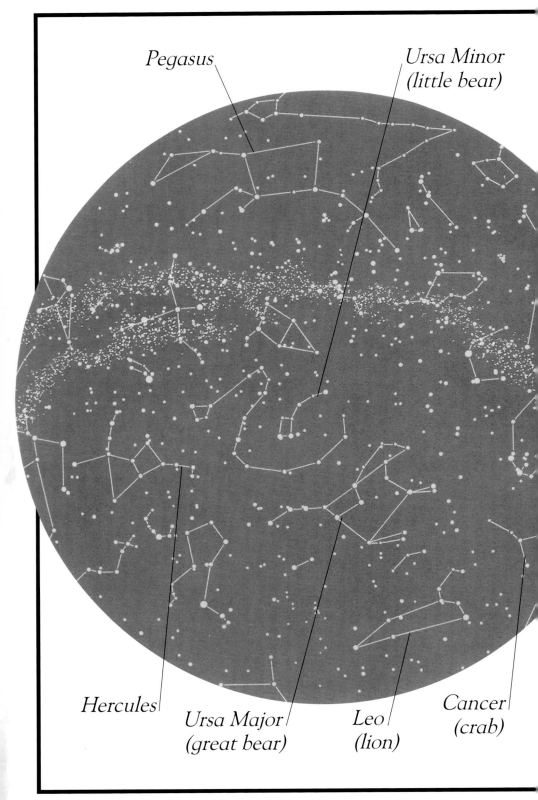

Pegasus

Ursa Minor
(little bear)

Hercules

Ursa Major
(great bear)

Leo
(lion)

Cancer
(crab)

Big star patterns are
called constellations
[KON-stuh-lay-shunz].
Star maps help you find
the constellations.

They tell you what star patterns
you can see at different times
of the year.

Star maps also show you
the different stars you can see
in different parts of the world.

The zodiac

The zodiac is a band of
12 constellations, such
as Leo and Cancer,
that the Sun appears to
pass through in a year.

Cancer the crab

There are 88 named constellations.
Some are named after animals, birds, and fish.
Others have the names of people and creatures from legends.
There are some constellations named after objects, such as crowns and cups.
The names help people locate stars in the night sky.

Corona
[kuh-ROW-nuh]
the crown

Ursa Minor

Pegasus

Cancer

Leo

Ursa Major

Hercules

9

The Big Dipper

*The Ursa Major
constellation*

Many constellations have animal names, such as Ursa Major [ER-suh MAY-jer] the great bear, Leo the lion, and Lupus the wolf. The constellation Taurus [TOR-us] shows the front of a bull. Bulls were important symbols for people in ancient times.

The Big Dipper
A star pattern called the Big Dipper, or the Plow, links seven bright stars in Ursa Major.

The Taurus constellation

Apis [AY-pus], the Ancient Egyptian bull god

They made statues of them and worshipped them as gods.

11

*The Pleiades
star cluster on
the shoulder of
Taurus*

*The seven sisters
called the Pleiades*

Different cultures tell different
star stories.

In a Greek legend, the hunter
Orion chased seven sisters called
the Pleiades [PLEE-uh-deez].

The girls escaped from him
by turning into doves.
Finally, they became stars.

Navajo [NA-vuh-ho] Indians
call these seven stars
the Flint Boys.
Their sky god, Black God,
wore them on his ankle.
When he stamped
his foot, they bounced
onto his forehead
and stayed there.

The Flint Boys

*Navajo drawing
of Black God*

Orion [oh-RYE-un] the hunter is another well-known constellation. He carries a club, and a sword hangs from his belt.
Nearby is his hunting dog— the constellation Canis Major [KAY-nus MAY-jer] the great dog. The brightest star Sirius [SEER-ee-us], or the Dog Star, is found in this constellation.

Sirius

The Canis Major constellation

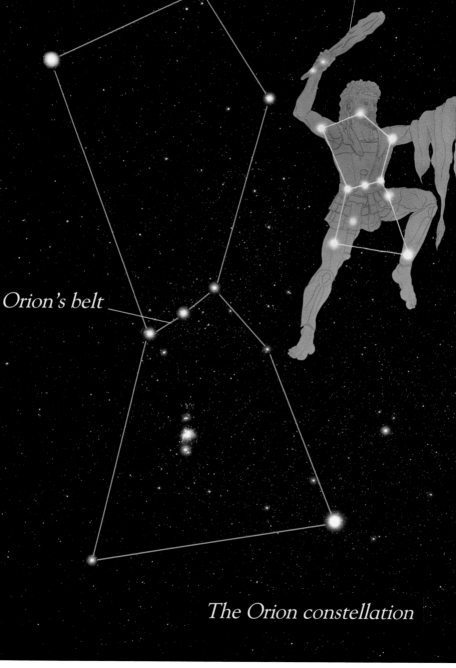

Orion the hunter

Orion's belt

The Orion constellation

Cepheus
[SEE-fee-us]

Cassiopeia
[kass-ee-oh-PEE-uh]

Perseus
[PURR-see-us]

Andromeda
[an-DRAH-muh-duh]

The W-shaped constellation is
called Cassiopeia.

In a Greek story, she is the wife
of King Cepheus and they have
a daughter named Andromeda.

*Perseus killing
the sea monster Cetus*

Andromeda was chained to
a rock, waiting to be eaten by
the sea monster Cetus [SEE-tus].
The Greek hero Perseus flew down
on the winged horse, Pegasus, and
saved Andromeda.

Pegasus [PEG-uh-sus]
The winged horse, Pegasus,
appears in many Greek
stories. He was shown
on Ancient Greek coins,
vases, and other objects.

Earth is more than one million times smaller than the Sun.

Faraway stars look small
and vary in brightness.
Close-up, they are enormous,
fiery balls of gas.
The Sun is our nearest star.
Explosions in the Sun's scorching
core make it shine.

Huge flares jumping into space from the Sun

Star colors

The hottest stars are blue and the coolest are red. In between are white, yellow, and orange stars.

The sizzling surface simmers like milk bubbling in a saucepan. Heat and light escape into space from the surface.

*In our galaxy, the Sun is
in one of the spiral arms.*

Most stars belong to giant
star groups called galaxies.
The Sun is one of at least
100 billion stars in
the Milky Way galaxy.
This galaxy has a spiral shape.

There are many
other galaxies
in the universe.
Some are spiral
with a bar of stars across the middle.
Others are shaped like tadpoles,
rings, or even Mexican hats!

Sombrero (Mexican
hat) galaxy

Barred-spiral galaxy

Ring galaxy

Tadpole galaxy

A Chinese story says that the star Vega [VEE-guh] was Chih Nu, the gods' weaving girl, and the star Altair was Niu Lang, a cowherd. When Chih Nu married Niu Lang, the angry gods separated them with a river, the Milky Way.

The Milky Way
From Earth, our galaxy is seen on its side. The light from the distant stars looks like a river of milk.

Vega

The Milky Way
separates the
two stars.

Altair

On Chinese Valentine's Day,
the Milky Way appears dimmer.
On this one day, Chih Nu
and Niu Lang are not separated.

The Eagle

Altair is found in the constellation of Aquila [A-kwuh-luh] the eagle. This bird belonged to the Greek god Zeus.

Altair

Altair, Vega, and a star called Deneb form the Summer Triangle. Deneb is 25 times larger and shines 60,000 times stronger than the Sun.

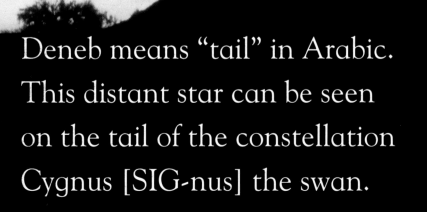

Deneb
The Cygnus constellation
Vega

Deneb means "tail" in Arabic. This distant star can be seen on the tail of the constellation Cygnus [SIG-nus] the swan.

Stars have often helped people
in their daily lives.
In Egypt, people realized that
when the star Sirius rose before
the Sun in summer, the Nile River
would soon flood.
They needed the flood for growing
healthy crops in their fields.

A traveler finding his position from a star

In the past, sailors and other travelers used special tools to look at stars so they could check their position and find their way.

Starry signposts
Two stars in the Southern Cross point to the South Pole. The North Star is seen above the North Pole.

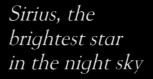

*Sirius, the
brightest star
in the night sky*

On a clear night we can see
thousands of stars, and with
special equipment we can see
even more.

Sirius seen through binoculars

Sirius seen through a strong telescope

With binoculars, we can see tens of thousands of stars. With a small telescope, we can see millions of stars. Astronomers—people who study the stars—use powerful telescopes.

Powerful telescopes have been put into space to discover more about the universe.
The Hubble Space Telescope orbits the Earth.
It provides very detailed images of faraway galaxies.

Hubble Space Telescope

Chandra X-ray Observatory

The Chandra X-ray Observatory picks up X-rays—light that is invisible to us—from the stars.

In the future, who knows what else we will discover in the mysterious starry sky. . .

Starry facts

There are more stars in the universe than grains of sand on all of the beaches on Earth.

Astronomers measure how far away stars are in light-years. A light-year is the distance light can travel in a year—about 5.88 trillion miles (9 trillion km). The star Sirius is eight and a half light-years away.

A shooting star is not really a star. It is actually a meteor, a piece of comet dust falling from space.

An observatory is where astronomers observe the night sky. In the mountains of Chile, where the skies are very clear, four separate telescopes work together to get amazing images of the universe.

A planisphere is a star map that has a rotating window. The window is lined up with the date and time of night to show the stars that can be seen.

Index